I0115773

WHAT DOES IT MEAN TO BE HUMAN IN THE AFTERMATH OF HISTORICAL TRAUMA?

Re-envisioning The Sunflower and why Hannah Arendt was wrong

Pumla Gobodo-Madikizela

THE NORDIC AFRICA INSTITUTE
AND UPPSALA UNIVERSITY
UPPSALA 2016

INDEXING TERMS:

Reparative humanism
Ubuntu
Empathic repair
Remorse
Forgiveness

What does it mean to be human in the aftermath of historical trauma?
Re-envisioning The Sunflower and why Hannah Arendt was wrong

ISBN 978-91-7106-788-3

© 2016 The author, The Nordic Africa Institute and Uppsala University

Cover photo: Alexandra, a township on the far outskirts of Johannes-
burg, South Africa in the time of Apartheid, 1982, UN Photo/DB.

Layout: Henrik Alfredsson, The Nordic Africa Institute
Print on demand: Lightning Source UK Ltd.

The opinions expressed in this volume are those of the author and
do not necessarily reflect the views of the Nordic Africa Institute nor
Uppsala University.

This book is made available as a printed book, as an e-book
and as a pdf-book under a Creative Commons Attribution-Non Com-
mercial-No Derivatives 4.0 International (CC BY-NC-ND 4.0) Licence.
Further details regarding permitted usage can be found
at www.creativecommons.org/licenses/by-nc-nd/4.0

Contents

Editor's Preface

During the fall of 2015, Dr. Pumla Gobodo-Madikizela, Professor at Stellenbosch University in South Africa, was the 12th distinguished scholar from an African university to hold the Claude Ake Visiting Chair in Uppsala, since its inauguration in 2003. At the end of her much appreciated stay in Uppsala, as it is always requested of the holders of this chair, she gave a lecture in memory of Professor Claude Ake, the distinguished scholar, philosopher, teacher and humanist, in whose honor the chair was set up. This report is the printed version of this lecture, given in Uppsala on December 9, 2015.

In her lecture, Dr. Gobodo-Madikizela discussed the importance of dealing with deep human traumas, starting from the writings of Simon Wiesenthal and Hannah Arendt and relating this in a most fruitful way to the experience of the TRC, the Truth and Reconciliation Commission of South Africa, a commission where she herself served on the Human Rights Violations Committee from 1995 to 1998. In particular, she focused on the personal confrontations between victims and perpetrators, giving a sharp context for the issue of forgiveness.

This lecture is important for students of African affairs, as it combines ethics and psychology, politics and philosophy. It is a great honor to be able to include Dr. Pumla Gobodo-Madikizela's contribution in this series of distinguished lectures.

As is customary to note, this publication constitutes the work of the author and does not necessarily reflect the views of the host institutions.

Uppsala, Sweden, October 2016

Peter Wallensteen
Professor, Department of Peace and Conflict Research, Uppsala University
Associate, Nordic Africa Institute
Editor, Claude Ake Memorial Papers Series (CAMP)

Thoughtless conformity is a problem that has been observed repeatedly in systematic crimes against humanity

Photos: National Photo Collection, the Israeli Government Press Office

The media interest in Eichmann's trial was enormous. When it began in April 1961, before the Jerusalem District Court, journalists from all over the world were there to cover the story. Among them Hannah Arendt, whose reporting for The New Yorker later evolved into the book *Eichmann in Jerusalem*, first published in 1963.

Background

In a well-known passage in *Eichmann in Jerusalem*, Hannah Arendt writes about the Nazi mass killer Eichmann, who was captured in Buenos Aires and tried for his Nazi crimes in Jerusalem:

> Eichmann was not Iago and not Macbeth... and nothing would have been farther from his mind than to determine, with Richard III, 'to prove a villain.' ... He merely, to put the matter colloquially, never realized what he was doing. ... It was sheer thoughtlessness – something by no means identical with stupidity – that predisposed him to become one of the greatest criminals of that period. ... That such ... thoughtlessness can wreak more havoc than all the evil instincts taken together ... was the lesson one could learn in Jerusalem.[1]

I am fully aware of the debates that have emerged since Arendt's statement about Eichmann's thoughtlessness – for instance critical objections by Joseph Beatty and Richard

---

1   Arendt, Hannah. 1994. Eichmann in Jerusalem: A report on the banality of evil. New York: Penguin.

Bernstein who question Arendt's argument about the link between thoughtlessness and the failure of moral reflection.[2, 3] However, I think that Arendt adequately elaborates on the significance of *thoughtlessness* in crimes against humanity in *Eichmann in Jerusalem* and in other publications such as *The Life of the Mind*.[4]

Thoughtless conformity is a problem that has been observed repeatedly in systematic crimes against humanity. Unable to engage reflectively about their actions, ordinary human beings become entangled in an "inextricable web of actions," as d'Entrèves characterises the behavior that contributes to cruelty and unspeakable forms of violence against others.[5] Young-Bruehl, Hannah Arendt's biographer, has argued that the capacity to "stop thinking," grew out of the unquestioning support for Hitler's "vision of the glorious Thousand Year Reich" by the German population.[6] Under "conditions of terror," Arendt informs us, most people "will comply" with the most evil policies of a totalitarian regime, as shown by the total lack of resistance by the German population at large to Hitler's extermination policies and the deportation of the Jews in Nazi Germany.[7]

What this means is that culpability for crimes against humanity does not only rest with the individual perpetrators who committed the crimes in question. Rather, the question of complicity turns the spotlight on the broader public – those whose votes and other kinds of active or silent support contributed to the flourishing of oppressive regimes. It focuses attention on the broader framework of the political-ideological context that fostered an environment in which dehumanization and gross human rights violations thrived. This component of crimes against humanity, the one that resides at the systemic, institutional and social levels rather than at an individual level, leads me to suggest that in the aftermath of historical trauma, restoring human bonds requires a new vocabulary of re-humanization. This new mode of being human, what I have referred to as "reparative humanism," opens towards a horizon of an ethics of care for the sake of a transformed society.[8]

If the level of depravity that has been captured most compellingly with the phrase "the banality of evil" is fostered in an environment in which inhumanity against others thrives, then it should be possible that relationships that foster thoughtfulness and a sense of being human reproduce themselves in our relational world.[9]

---

2   Beatty, Joseph. 1994. "Thinking and moral considerations: Socrates and Arendt's Eichmann." In *Hannah Arendt: Critical Essays*, edited by L. P. Hinchman & S. K. Hinchman, 57-78. Albany: State University of New York Press.

3   Bernstein, Richard. 2000. "Arendt on thinking." In *The Cambridge companion to Hannah Arendt* edited by D. Villa, 277-291. United Kingdom: Cambridge University Press.

4   Arendt, Hannah. 1981. *The Life of the Mind*. New York: Houghton Mifflin Harcourt.

5   D'Entrèves, Maurizio P. 1994. *The Political Philosophy of Hannah Arendt*. London and New York: Routledge.

6   Young-Bruehl, Elisabeth. 2009. *Why Arendt Matters*. New Haven: Yale University Press.

7   Arendt, *Eichmann in Jerusalem*, 233.

8   Gobodo-Madikizela, Pumla. 2010. "Reconciliation: A Call to Reparative Humanism." In *In the Balance: South Africans Debate Reconciliation*, edited by F. du Toit & E. Doxtade, 133-139. Cape Town: Jacana.

9   Arendt, *Eichmann in Jerusalem*.

This essay is inspired by the question: in dealing with the past, including its transgenerational repercussions, how can we create moral spaces that would allow the imagining of relationships that bestow a sense of worth on others in ways that were not possible before? I do so by exploring examples from unique historical moments that have been illuminating. These examples are less from the great philosophers and religious or political theorists than from ordinary people who themselves have suffered irreparably. The lessons from these historical moments show that there is something to learn about what is possible in human behaviour in the aftermath of genocide and mass political violence. My exploration begins with the Truth and Reconciliation Commission (TRC) of South Africa. In dealing with the complexity of the transitional period after the fall of apartheid, and with the question of what the appropriate response to gross human rights violations should be when victims, perpetrators and bystanders live in the same country, the TRC opened up new avenues of inquiry. It also inspired debates about turning away from violence towards a new post-colonial and post-apartheid ethics that could help build, in the words of Frantz Fanon, a more human "world of the *You*".[10]

---

10 Fanon, Frantz. 1967. Black Skin, White Masks. New York: Grove Press.

Archbishop Desmond Tutu and Professor Pumla Gobodo-Madikizela at the University of the Free State, Bloemfontein, in October 2013. Gobodo-Madikizela and Tutu worked closely together in the 1990's at the Truth and Reconciliation Commission (TRC) of South Africa. She served the TRC as a Human Rights Committee member from 1995 to 1998, during which time he headed the Commission.

The Truth and Reconciliation Commission: A New Norm of Recognition

The hope that Nelson Mandela inspired in the aftermath of apartheid was grounded in the quest to establish a richer sense of identity that would connect all South Africans as members of a human community. Mandela expanded the horizon of what is possible in human relationships by spearheading, as part of the political negotiations, a process of dialogue. This was aimed at fostering a capacity for connecting with former enemies, in order to confront and heal a past characterized by moral corruption and widespread violations of human rights. The TRC broke new ground not because it was the first of its kind. Rather, it was because the TRC was unique in many ways, not least because of the public expressions of remorse by perpetrators of gross human rights violations, and the scenes of victims forgiving perpetrators. This essay reflects on this unique dimension of the South African story. It seeks to examine the empathic movement that draws victim and villain towards a shared vision of a world in which the Other matters, and to explore the foundational role of empathy in this movement towards the Other and its expression in remorse and forgiveness.

By its very nature, and as a quasi-judicial process, the TRC was a dialogic space with the potential to produce emergent forms of subjectivity that opened up the possibility of transformation. The TRC transformed the silence of trauma – the wordless speech of trauma – and restored victims' sense of agency by providing an environment in which victims were able to break their silence in front of a national audience. Being recognized leads to the experience of healthy subjectivity. In a society emerging from political conflict, where the rules of recognition were written into the laws of a repressive state, Black people's subject position was bound up with norms of subordination and misrecognition.

In contrast, the norms of recognition established by the TRC were based on a new set of principles that restored victims' sense of agency. These included, among others, acknowledgment and a "sense of affirmation and validation that is so crucial to victims of trauma," testifying from the standpoint of their own authorship in the presence of a community in which perpetrators were required to give full public disclosure and to confess their crimes.[11]

Narrating traumatic memory from the public stage of the TRC may be one way that victims and survivors attempt to reconstruct a shattered self, transcend the passivity of victimhood, and find a voice to construct meaning from their traumatic experience. By making their wounds public, recording the atrocities visited on them, and identifying the perpetrators, their testimonies helped both to assert and restore their sense of agency. This took various forms.

One anti-apartheid activist, who had been raped multiple times and tortured during detention, described her unbearable experiences. She told the TRC audience that in order to shut out the pain and shame she would "remove" her soul from her body and put it in a corner so that the rape was "only" on her body. Appealing to the restorative possibilities of the TRC, she expressed the wish that the commission would help her get her soul back.[12]

Another witness, Owen McGregor, wrote his testimony in his dead brother's "voice," explaining that the words were what he thought his brother would have said had he, Owen, been the one who died. His brother, Wallace, was killed when he served as a conscript under the South African Defence Force fighting the forces of liberation in Namibia before its independence in 1989. In the testimony, Wallace, speaking through his brother, accused the apartheid government leaders of lying to the young white men who forced to serve in the army: he asked, "Why did I die?" Giving a dead person a voice – entering the silence of the grave – is quite profound in symbolism. It is a kind of sacrificial act: trading places with one's brother and "dying" in his place. Owen McGregor's testimony was as much about maintaining a sense of attachment to his brother's memory as it was an attempt at working through his own loss. The testimony of their mother, Anne-Marie McGregor, about her anguish at not being able to see her son's face for the last time when his body was brought home for burial in a body bag, was presented at the end of the first TRC session of the day, just before the morning tea break. During the break, a group of Black women who had testified earlier about the brutal killing of their sons by security police took turns in reaching out and embracing Mrs. McGregor. I asked one of the women what motivated this show of compassion, and she replied, "None of us ever had reason to embrace a white person before, but this was an instinctive act, you know, a mother-to-mother feeling." Another woman explained, "We know what losing a loved one means. She seemed so alone – we just couldn't help it."[13]

---

11   Gobodo-Madikizela, "Remorse, forgiveness and rehumanization."
12   Facing the Truth with Bill Moyers. Film. New York: Gail Pellett, 1999.
13   Ngewu, Cynthia. Interview by Pumla Gobodo-Madikizela. Research Interview. Cape Town, April 1997.

The complex field of relational encounters and the possibilities unfolding at public hearings of the TRC extended far beyond the actual stage of TRC hearings. It encompassed the wider audience "present" as witnesses to what was happening on the national stage through the live broadcast of the testimonies, and through the weekly-televised programs that re-presented the trauma testimonies. Elsewhere I have used the metaphor "making public spaces intimate" to describe how the internal and external overlapping of a matrix of emotions and memories in the TRC fostered the emergence of new forms of subjectivity extending to a much wider terrain than the audience actually present at the hearings.[14] The power of this broader relational context in the wider social milieu paved the way for a range of identifications and reciprocal influences that are difficult to imagine in prosecutorial responses to historical trauma (e.g., the Nuremberg trials in the aftermath of the Holocaust). The TRC approach was unique in that by adopting an invitational stance – rather than an adversarial one – perpetrators were asked to "give full disclosure" of the crimes they committed in exchange for amnest.[15] Without the threat of punishment, and with the promise of amnesty for truth telling, perpetrators were inspired to admit guilt rather than disown it. Thus, it was possible to face and, for some at least, to feel their guilt. This is an important distinction, because one can simply "face up" to what one has done, acknowledging it at an intellectual level, without taking responsibility for the horrific deeds committed, and instead externalizing blame. It is as if the person were saying, "I give you what you want, full disclosure. Here is the list of evil deeds in which I participated under orders."

In contrast, feeling the burden of guilt goes beyond acknowledgment to recognize that one's actions have caused injury and led to a rupture in one's human community, and that by the very fact of one's participation in those acts, one excluded oneself from the realm of humanity. It is this recognition of alienation from the bonds of human community, and a deep sense of guilt about it – a feeling of brokenness at one's inner core of humanness – that makes remorse – an emotion that makes perpetrators quintessentially human – possible. Perpetrators' subject position of guilt for the crimes they committed – rather than the position of innocence "until proven guilty" – is the context within which a new perpetrator subjectivity unfolds, one that seeks integration of the uncomfortable reality within the self at a deeper internal level. Remorse can be a painful affect, because it involves facing the past and its uncomfortable and internally unsettling truths. Remorse is also an important moment of recognition of the pain that the perpetrator's actions have caused the victim. It is, in other words, an expression of the perpetrator's empathic response to the victim's pain.

---

14 Gobodo-Madikizela, Pumla. 2008. "Trauma, forgiveness and the witnessing dance: Making public spaces intimate." Journal of Analytic Psychology 53: 169-188.

15 Promotion of National Unity and Reconciliation Act 34 of 1995, paragraph (a), subsection (3), section 20.

Victims' Intersubjective Encounter with Perpetrators' Empathy

The psychoanalytic explanation of empathy opens up interesting possibilities for understanding the dynamics of forgiveness. The psychoanalyst Heinz Kohut defined empathy as "the capacity to think and feel oneself into the inner life of another person".[16] Other definitions of empathy are aligned with this view of empathic responsiveness (e.g., Daniel Stern's "affect attunement").[17] The essence of empathy is the capacity to feel with and to participate in shared reflective engagement with the other's inner life. Most scholars recognize some form of identification with the other at a deeper internal level as central to the capacity for empathy. Merleau-Ponty, for example, defined empathy as "the intertwining of our lives with those of others".[18] For David Black, empathy involves a process of imagination. It is "a sophisticated act of the imagination, a 'trial identification' done by someone who is consciously relating to another's mental state".[19]

An aspect of empathy that has received scant scholarly attention is the component of care for the other that sometimes emerges in the context of empathic responsiveness. Caring goes beyond "mirroring" or feeling into the mental state of another. It arises from the moment-by-moment negotiation of the intersubjective relationship between actors, as well as from introspection and ongoing mutual reflection, and it involves making sense of the intersubjective experience of empathic resonance. In this desire-to-care-for-the-other aspect of empathy, the empathic response of the victim is imbued with a quality of wishing to "rescue" the remorseful perpetrator, as if to affirm his identity as a member of the human community (instead of a "monster" or "evil one"). This desire to rescue the perpetrator, I argue, constitutes the fundamental moment, a pivotal point in the intersubjective context in which forgiving feelings emerge.

The word *forgiveness*, is the wrong word for describing what unfolds in these victim-perpetrator encounters. Forgiveness seems to suggest a fixed position, or a coming to an end – "I offer you forgiveness so that I can have closure and move on." There is a subtext here that seems to signify an act of leaving something behind, moving on without looking back. This is evocative of the notion of "letting go" in the stages theory of forgiveness advocated by Robert Enright and his colleagues.[20] The notion of "letting go" has also been used in psychoanalytic explications of forgiveness, with some

16   Kohut, Heinz. 1984. How does analysis cure? Chicago: University of Chicago Press.
17   Stern, Daniel N. 2004. The first relationship: Infant and mother. Cambridge: Havard University Press, 2004.
18   Merleau-Ponty, Maurice. 1968. The visible and the invisible. Evanston Ill.: Northwestern University Press.
19   Black, David. 2004. "Sympathy reconfigured: Some reflections on sympathy, empathy and the discovery of values." International Journal of Psycho-Analysis 85: 579-95.
20   Enright, Robert and North, Joanna. 1998. Exploring forgiveness. Wisconsin: University of Wisconsin Press.

psychoanalytic scholars associating letting go with the process of mourning. However, if we consider the movement toward a forgiving attitude as inspired by mourning, then forgiveness should be seen as a transition, as a working through of the pain, suffering and loss caused by trauma on the part of victims, and working through of a range of losses on the part of perpetrators along with the emotions that emerge after confronting one's guilt and shame. Accordingly, a characteristic of this process of "working through" is the integration of disparate aspects of one's self- and the representations of these aspects of the self in one's internal world. These aspects must be owned as part of the self, the loss that brought about the rupture must be mourned, and the transition to forgiveness must be worked through. Something else grows in the place of whatever it was that prevented connection to the other – anger, resentment, desire for revenge, etc. "Letting go" does not capture this subtlety.

Perhaps what takes place in victim-perpetrator encounters is "the emergence of the unexpected."[21] A certain degree of caring for the other evolves from being witnesses to each other's pain – the "witnessing dance" that brings survivor and perpetrator into step with each other, into the spiral movement of a new intersubjective context that edges them toward the centre of possibility, and then upward toward the apex of transformation.[22] The new intersubjective context that emerges allows for integration and containment, rather than "letting go." Acknowledgment that bears responsibility, that conveys compassion and care, and that is prepared to enter the pain of the other: this is what is crucial for this transformative process.

An example that illustrates this idea of expression of care beyond empathic resonance is the response of Linda and Peter Biehl to their daughter Amy's killers after their appearance at the TRC Amnesty hearings.[23] Amy Biehl was a Stanford University student on a Fulbright scholarship in South Africa. She was stabbed to death when, as part of her work with a non-profit organization, she visited a Black township in Cape Town with her colleagues from the non-profit. Her killers' remorseful submission to the TRC led Linda and Peter Biehl to support their amnesty application. When the TRC granted amnesty to the men, Peter and Linda Biehl arranged skills training for them and offered them positions in the Amy Biehl Foundation, which they had established in their daughter's memory. "I have no hatred in my heart," Linda said in an interview I conducted with her and her husband. "All I am concerned about is how these young men can re-enter their community and rebuild their lives."[24]

As I have noted in my work, this kind of response presents a paradox. Yet it is this stance of hearing the perpetrator's desire – expressed through remorse – for readmission into the world of shared moral humanity, and a caring-enough, that helps sustain

21 Gobodo-Madikizela, Pumla. 2016. "Interrupting cycles of repetition: Creating spaces for dialogue, facing and mourning the past." In Breaking intergenerational cycles of repetition: A global dialogue on historical trauma and memory, edited by Pumla Gobodo-Madikizela, 113-134. Toronto: Barbara Budrich Publishers.

22 Gobodo-Madikizela, "Trauma, forgiveness and the witnessing dance."

23 Truth and Reconciliation Commission Amnesty Hearing. Cape Town, 8 July 1997.

24 Biehl, Linda. Interview by Pumla Gobodo-Madikizela. Research Interview. Cape Town, April 1998.

the perpetrator's remorse and prevents disintegration. I am beginning to think about this act or "gesture" of caring on the part of victims in terms of the psychoanalytic object relations notion of a "position."[25] It is a position that goes beyond forgiveness, and it serves two possible functions. First, it seeks to "restore" the survival of the lost loved one who was murdered by the perpetrator. Second, by showing the kind of caring and containment that can help prevent disintegration in the perpetrator, the victim creates a new relational experience with him, which reconstitutes the memory of the loss as a positive narrative.

The "caring-for" element in empathy is the result of a deeper level of imagination and understanding of the other's experience. This deeper level of imagination takes "feeling into" the mental state of the other to another level, and asks the question, *What should I do about it?* Thus, rather than empathy considered simply as "resonance," the notion of "empathic repair" might usefully be applied to capture the transformation and potential for healing that emerge from dialogic encounters between survivors and perpetrators.[26] The perpetrator's transformation stands as a symbol of the victim's capacity (and, more generally, of the human capacity) for imagination and understanding, and of the power of empathic care that is inherent – always a potentiality[27] – in dialogic encounters between victims and perpetrators.

These unique moments of encounter between family members of victims and perpetrators invite us seriously to consider new possibilities that were unimaginable before. The TRC has presented us with new solutions that dared to transcend the "limits" of the human condition, challenging the notion that prosecutorial justice is the only rational stance. Hanna Arendt, for example, writes in her book *The Human Condition* that acts of radical evil "transcend the realm of human affairs" and are therefore neither punishable nor forgivable. Radically evil deeds, she argues, are unpunishable because no amount of punishment can restore a sense of symmetry that would balance what they have done. They are unforgivable because no yardstick exists by which we can measure what it means to forgive them, and there is no mental disposition we can adopt toward them that would correct the sense of injustice that their actions have injected into our world. In light of what we have witnessed at the South African TRC, as well as reconciliation efforts in countries trying to restore the ruptured soul of their communities after wars and genocide, however, a critical reflection on the limits of Arendt's, and other scholars who have advanced philosophical explanations of the idea of the "unforgiveable" is necessary.

---

25 The psychoanalytic object relations theorist Melanie Klein referred to certain early developmental mental states as "positions" that describe the state of mind that accrues from the constellation of complex feelings that play out in the internal world as well as externally in mother-infant interactions. The notion of "position" as I use it here connotes the reflective engagement that occurs in victim-perpetrator dialogue that allows movement from one position – such as resentment – to another. The dynamics that operate in this transformative process are inspired by the capacity for reflection – the opposite of "thoughtlessness" – which enables the connection with the feelings of another person.

26 Gobodo-Madikizela, Pumla. 2008. "Empathetic repair after mass trauma: When vengeance is arrested." European Journal of Social Theory 11: 331-350.

27 Young-Bruehl, Why Arendt Matters, 4-5.

Philosophical thought has been useful in defining an ethics of forgiveness, setting a "standard" for what is forgivable, and what is unforgivable – unclear though this standard may be. The line between, on the one hand, what lies beyond the purview of forgiveness – that which is impossible to forgive – and on the other hand, what is in principle unforgivable is not always clear in these philosophical debates. The practice of forgiveness, its possibility in a range of situations in political life, cannot be addressed only by an understanding of ethics. Philosophical thought cannot explain how forgiveness happens, what conditions are necessary for it to occur when it does occur, why some people choose to forgive perpetrators of terrible crimes while others find it difficult to forgive these crimes.

These limits to philosophical discourse apply also to legal perspectives as well as to notions of forgiveness advanced in Arendtian political thought. One of the problem with these views, which have come to represent conventional wisdom on the subject of forgiveness in some circles, is that they are no longer realistic in light of actual practice in post-conflict situations in the present generation. Many intractable conflicts have not been resolved by the application of the strict rule of law, which advocates prosecutions for perpetrators of politically motivated atrocities. Cycles of violent conflict tend to reproduce themselves, turning victims into perpetrators in an unending vicious cycle of repetition of vengeful violence and hatred. In the book *An Ethic for Enemies: Forgiveness in Politics*, social ethicist Donald Shriver describes forgiveness as "a collective turning from the past that neither ignores past evil nor excuses it ... [and that] insists on the humanity of enemies ...."[28] Strategies of restoring peace and social cohesion after political conflict are driven by the hope that some form of transformation in individuals, groups and societies will emerge because of post-conflict dialogue between former adversaries. Part of the goal of "dealing with the past" is to find the best approach that will help transform relationships in a society with a past marked by violent conflict between groups.

---

28   Donald W. Shriver Jr., An Ethic for Enemies: Forgiveness in Politics (New York, Oxford University Press, 1995) at 9.

Towards the Horizon of an Ethics of Care

Two examples of past atrocities illustrate that transformative possibilities may also be seen as pointing to a more general horizon of an ethics of care and responsibility for the other in the context of "dealing with the past."

Simon Wiesenthal's Encounter with Dying Nazi SS Soldier

Simon Wiesenthal was a survivor of the Nazi death camps who dedicated his life to hunting down Nazi perpetrators and documenting the crimes they committed. His book, *The Sunflower,* recounts the story of his encounter, when he was a camp inmate, with a dying SS soldier who asked for his forgiveness. In the book, Wiesenthal also describes his search for the home of the SS soldier and meeting his mother. Wiesenthal's book has paved the way for us to explore the question of what it means to be human in the aftermath of Nazi-era crimes in a way that has not been possible before. He has passed on to our generation, the post-Holocaust generation, the responsibility not simply to ponder the question of whether he was right or wrong not to forgive Karl, the SS man, but rather to reflect on the question of what it means to be human in the face of the aftermath of absolute evil. His book is unique in that his account reveals the potential for human connection in even the most unspeakably tragic circumstances. His narration of his conversation with Karl's mother captures these extraordinarily human moments. At one point in his account of meeting Karl's mother, he tells readers that he could not shatter "this broken woman's image of her son as A "good boy": "I took my leave," Wiesenthal writes, "without diminishing in any way the poor woman's last surviving consolation – faith in the goodness of her son".[29]

In the aftermath of the words-defying destruction and catastrophe in which Wiesenthal's loved ones were murdered, he demonstrated a sense of caring for the feelings of the "Other" despite the deep chasm that separated their worlds. This to me conveys, without any doubt, the empathy that the mother's grief evoked in him. These moments in Wiesenthal's journey with Karl the mass killer's story allow us to explore new avenues of inquiry that bear relevance to the moral question that Wiesenthal articulates for us in *The Sunflower.* The profound example of Wiesenthal's compassion for Karl's mother compels us to consider the question of what dynamics might drive victims towards empathy, and lead them to enter into a constructive encounter with the "Other," even when their internal moral compass points toward its inappropriateness and the "Other" seems morally undeserving.

Over the years, there have been many responses to Wiesenthal's dilemma that maintain a stance of certainty about the response that he ought or ought not to have given regarding the question of forgiveness. When he asked his friend Josek, with whom he

---

29   Wiesenthal, Simon. 1998. The Sunflower: On the Possibilities and Limits of Forgiveness. New York: Schocken Books.

was in the death camp, whether he did the right thing by not forgiving the SS man, Josek told him he had no right to forgive on behalf of the dead. Yet Wiesenthal continued to wrestle with his decision to keep his silence and walk away. The fact that his response evoked moral questions for him, which, as he writes, "challenged my heart and my mind" long after his encounter with the young SS man, and leading to relentless reflection on the question whether he did the right thing, suggests that the dying Karl's words affected him.[30] This is what struck me the most about Wiesenthal's *Sunflower* book story when I first read it. He did not respond with the kind of revulsion that might be expected after meeting a person who participated in the atrocity of the Holocaust, and dismiss the encounter with Karl as one that is unworthy of any further reflection. Rather, Wiesenthal continued to engage with it and to challenge us to put ourselves in his shoes, and for each of us to ask the question: What would I have done?

Reading *The Sunflower* in the twenty-first century, when the language of "dealing with the past" has been dominated by dialogue between perpetrators of atrocities who live in the same country as the victims of their crimes, I find it difficult to respond to the question posed in Wiesenthal's book only by using the lens of moral judgment.

A question often raised by scholars and religious leaders who have been invited to participate in the seminars organised around Wiesenthal's dilemma concerns whether Karl the SS man cared for Wiesenthal as an individual who had lost loved ones in the Holocaust destruction. The discussion of this issue has led some to conclude that Karl's quest was a selfish one, because he seemed to see Wiesenthal as an "anonymous other" – the Jew that he had asked a nurse to find for him.

At the same time however, one could argue that Karl recognised that Jewish people suffered the Nazi machinery of unspeakable destruction collectively, and that the crime he committed was a crime directed at Jews as a people. Therefore, it may be significant that Karl asked the nurse to call "a Jew." Seeking connection with a living human victim, however, seems to suggest a desire for something else that went beyond forgiveness. I suggest that this something else was a hopeless hope to "repair" the irreparable legacy of brokenness he was about to leave behind. Like remorse, his was an act of accountability, facing his guilt and recognising that his actions caused a rupture in the human community beyond repair.

Yet more than remorse, he may have wanted confirmation of his *human beingness*. In other words, he needed a witness to guide him in his search, albeit a hopeless search, to reclaim a sense of humanity lost in the countless acts of mass murders he committed. His last wish, I argue, was granted. More than seven decades after Karl the SS man asked Wiesenthal to forgive him, he continues to live in Wiesenthal's memory not as one of the evil SS officers who died in German army hospitals, but as Karl who challenged a Jew's heart and mind with his words of repentance for many decades to come. His story, retold by Wiesenthal as its only witness is a poignant one – the message equally poignant – as it continues to inspire debate about what the appropriate response to the remorse of perpetrators of atrocities and historical trauma should be – about how

---

30   Ibid.

we might be able to reclaim our sense of being human in the aftermath of unspeakable crimes against humanity.

In thinking about this story, one is inclined to ask, what motivates the need to face the victim (as Karl did), or to search out the mother of the perpetrator (as Wiesenthal did)? Granted, sometimes there are clearly stated motivations, (to find out "the truth", to ask for forgiveness, etc.). Yet it seems to me that there is more at play. The "more" is a tacit recognition that healing must involve the "Other," is dependent on the "Other." While victim and perpetrator are separated by their pasts, at the same time, their past also connects them, opening up a potential space for the emergence of unexpected human moments. At the second and third generation level, the dialogue about the past should be transformed into a facilitative environment, inspiring an ethical impulse that may open a window for expression of acknowledgement and facing inherited shame and guilt on the part of perpetrators' descendants, and acceptance and survivors' desire to rebuild new human bonds or to restore old ones.

The task then points to the importance of a deeper level of recognition, one that goes beyond acknowledgment (which may at times simply recognize the other as a mere object). Reciprocal recognition of the other's humanity, acknowledging the reality of each other's pain and suffering, whatever its source, is the kind of empathy that creates pathways to caring for the other as a fellow human being. Such empathic responses have also been observed in the case of family members of victims responding with care and concern for the welfare of perpetrators.

The words of Cynthia Ngewu, whose son Christopher Piet was lured into a death trap by a black police collaborator, along with six other young men from the Gugulethu Township in Cape Town, South Africa (they came to be known as the Gugulethu Seven), crystallises this point.[31]

I had organised a public dialogue event on reconciliation on the side-lines of the TRC hearings in Cape Town. In response to a question I asked Mrs Ngewu, she explained her position on reconciliation: "This thing called reconciliation – if I am understanding it correctly – if it means that this man who killed Christopher has a chance to become human again, so that I, so that all of us... so that our humanity can be restored, then I agree with it. I support it."[32]

In considering the possibility of victims' empathy in these post-conflict encounters, it seems the human capacity for imagination plays a role, because imagination suggests constant reflection, co-construction of meaning, and dialogue with self and with the Other (as well as with internal "others") through language and other subtler forms of communication. The idea that empathy might involve imagination is perhaps best captured by the psychoanalyst Heinz Kohut's notion of "experience-near,"

---

31 Gobodo-Madikizela, Pumla. 2009. "Working Through the Past: Some Thoughts on Forgiveness in Cultural Context." In Memory, Narrative, and Forgiveness: Perspectives on the Unfinished Journeys of the Past, edited by Pumla Gobodo-Madikizela & Chris van der Merwe, 148-169. New Castle, UK: Cambridge Scholars Press.

32 Ngewu, Cynthia. Interview by Pumla Gobodo-Madikizela. Public dialogue event. Cape Town, November 1996.

which suggests an attempt to experience as closely as possible what the other person is experiencing – their pain, their sufferings.[33] It is an attempt, a reaching toward an experience not one's own in order to understand what *the other is going through*. In other words, the act of imagining is not only an approximation of the other's experience. It is the human intersubjectivity that develops from an ethical stance of mutual recognition and a capacity for moral imagination.

For Richard Kearney, "imagination is indispensable to ethics," a claim resting on what he regards as imagination's "empathic powers of receptivity to the other".[34] Kearney explains: "While the role of imagination in understanding pertains to its productive and projective powers, its role in sensible intuition expresses its ability *to remain open to what is given from beyond itself*" (my italics).[35]

What interests me most in this work is the question of what makes these encounters (between victims of historical trauma and those responsible for these traumas) even possible. It seems clear that once people, even those who are adversaries, are faced with each other, innumerable possibilities – both destructive and restorative and all that cannot be reduced to these oversimplified categories – arise, both 'within' and 'between' bodies. One can accept that those encountering each other will be *affected*. Whether they will be affected in a way that will move them to empathic understanding and new relational experience or to deeper empathic failures is another matter. The potential for the unexpected, unforeseen and thoroughly creative, endemic to the human condition is always present. Cromby for instance, writes of feelings:

> So feelings have no intrinsic capacity for progressive action, but their ontological
> status and concomitant irreducibility to the linguistic, the formally symbolic,
> gives them the continuous potential to be spatio-temporally disjunctive with any
> given 'rationality.' And it is these disjunctions, rather than their intrinsic qualities,
> that generate feelings' potential for creative disruption – just as their conjunctions
> generate their normative potentials.[36]

Earlier I suggested that a phrase that best describes the *process* of forgiveness is "the emergence of the unexpected." This idea captures Cromby's notion of feelings potential for creative *disruption* – the capacity for the emotional encounter with the other to open a new path, and to generate something completely unexpected. This second exemplar taken from the history of apartheid gross human rights violations illustrates the unexpected, "inexplicable," emotional responses that are sometimes evoked in encounters between victims and perpetrators.

---

33 Kohut, How does analysis cure, 187.
34 Kearney, Richard. 1993. Poetics of imagining: From Husserl to Lyotard. London: Routledge.
35 Ibid., 225.
36 Cromby, John. 2007. "Towards a psychology of feeling." International Journal of Critical Psychology 21: 94-118.

Young Woman Visits Mother's Killer in Prison and Forgives him, Supports his Parole Application

A second example is from the encounter between a young woman, Marcia Khoza, with her mother's killer, the apartheid government's chief assassin, Eugene de Kock, who was nicknamed "Prime Evil." After visiting de Kock in prison where he was serving his two life terms before he was granted parole, Marcia Khoza spoke publicly about forgiving him.

What does it mean to sit in the same room as the man who killed your mother, to face him and to engage him with questions about the killing? What did forgiving de Kock do for her – and for de Kock? What does it mean to forgive a man known as "Prime Evil," who, in the collective consciousness of South Africans is the embodiment of the evil of the apartheid system?

"I had this deep void of emptiness," Khoza said. "I carried so much anger to protect myself from falling into the abyss." Empowered by knowing the story of her mother's killing, and finally finding "the missing puzzle in the jigsaw of my life," as she described the experience, Marcia Khoza was able to mourn and to begin her healing journey. In recounting the story of her meeting with de Kock, she spoke about how meeting de Kock enabled her to empathise with him and his longing for his sons whom he told her he had not seen for more than twenty years.[37]

I asked her what was most memorable about the meeting with de Kock. She described a moment towards the end of the visit when she became conscious of her knees touching de Kock's under the narrow table across which they sat from each other in the prison. She was drawing closer and closer to him with each response he gave to her many questions, listening to the words, yet also listening to his "inner voice." At one point, she said, "I realised that our noses were almost touching, and that we were breathing the same air."

Breathing the same air – an ordinary statement, yet the extraordinary meaning it conveys transcends Marcia Khoza's story and enters the realm of the human universe. The statement brings into focus the emergent possibilities that are at the heart of these dialogic processes of restorative justice. In societies emerging from violent conflict, like South Africa, where victims, perpetrators, bystanders and beneficiaries of oppressive regimes live in the same country, and sometimes as neighbours, creating the space for such dialogue is an imperative.

As a metaphor, the notion of "breathing the same air" challenges the very concept of forgiveness. In considering encounters between survivors and perpetrators of gross human rights violations, what is perhaps necessary is shifting the lens from a focus on forgiveness and reconciliation (concepts that imply a goal) to "experience" (complicated, enigmatic, muddy, elusive, and unpredictable), because I think that much of what happens in these encounters remains implicit, and the word forgiveness falls short of adequately capturing this complexity.

---

37 Khoza, Marcia. Interview by Pumla Gobodo-Madikizela. Public dialogue event. Bloemfontein, December 2013.

Empathic Repair and the Spirit of Ubuntu

The need to build a world in which the Other matters is at the heart of my exploration in this paper. The trauma induced by years of violence need not lead to repetition of violence, where victims and their descendants become perpetrators of new forms of violence that play out in endless cycles of repetition. The pattern can be broken, the violence transformed and the trauma transcended. The work of the Truth and Reconciliation Commission (TRC) of South Africa reminds us that while it may not be possible to erase traumatic memory – "closure" after such violence and injustice is not possible – trauma's power of repetition can be broken.

In the aftermath of crimes against humanity, individuals and communities of survivors, and perpetrators who dare to face their shame and their guilt, and transcend it, are searching for ways of being human, for reconnection to their sense of agency, which is vital for a sense of being human. Perhaps a word that best captures what is needed is not forgiveness, but rather empathic repair. The notion of "empathic repair," points toward not only one's healing, but also one's responsibility to participate in the building of a society in which people could come together and be fellow human beings – "to touch the other, to feel the other" – sharing in the vision of a more humane society.[38] The TRC, the Rwandan gacaca process, and similar restorative justice processes[39] – all are strategies established to create a space for testimony, a space for confrontation and listening, for moral reflection and for initiating the difficult process of healing. These sites of testimony, of mutual recognition and shared experience, provide points of identification, entryways into the experience of others, which enable comparison across critical registers of difference. Appeal to the familiar and the familial creates a context in which it is possible to engage empathetic questions, such as "How old was your daughter/son when... ?" By grounding themselves in what is shared, they create mutual intelligibility. The shared experience of loss, for example, cuts across the distinction of black or white, Tutsi or Hutu, Israeli or Palestinian. On the terrain of a horrific past, certain statements resonate deeply: My son was eighteen years old when he was conscripted into the South African Defence Force during apartheid; he was brought back in a body bag and I wasn't allowed to see him." "My son was eighteen when he joined the anti-apartheid struggle. He was abducted, tortured, and killed by apartheid security police."

It is ironic that the same factors that can ignite and perpetuate animosity, fear, and hatred – the love for those killed or maimed by "the other" – might also suspend those negative sentiments. By providing a way into the experience of the "enemy," love and loss may provide a way out of violence. Ultimately, love and loss are what is common and thus in a sense is shared. Love and loss enable healing that opens new possibilities in the aftermath of violence.

---

38   Gobodo-Madikizela, "Empathetic repair after mass trauma: When vengeance is arrested."
39   Clark, Phil. 2010. The Gacaca Courts, Post-genocide Justice and Reconciliation in Rwanda: Justice without Lawyers. Cambridge: Cambridge University Press.

Gacaca court in Rwamagana district in Eastern Rwanda, 2006. Courts like this, inspired by traditional Rwandan communal justice systems, were adapted to fit the need for truth and reconciliation in Rwanda in the wake of the 1994 Genocide.

Photo: Elisa Finocchiaro, CC BY-NC 2.0

At the centre of this "love" is *ubuntu* – a deep sense of caring for the other that is embedded in most traditional African societies (see next two paragraphs for description of *ubuntu*). It is worth noting that the post-amble of the South African Interim Constitution of 1993, which outlined the guidelines for the establishment of the TRC, included a reference to "the need for ubuntu." This clearly conveyed a particular orientation for the work of the TRC, one that was specific to the South African cultural context.

The concept of *ubuntu* is an ethic based on the understanding that one's subjectivity is inextricably intertwined with that of others in one's community. From the perspective of *ubuntu*, all people are valued as part of the human community and worthy of being so recognized. This entails not blind acceptance of others, no matter what they do, but rather an orientation of openness to others and a reciprocal caring that fosters a sense of solidarity. *Ubuntu* is often associated with the concept of self "I am because we are," which stands in contrast to the Cartesian "I think, therefore I am." While recognizing the role of the individual, *ubuntu* values a sense of solidarity with others – the individual always in relation – rather than individual autonomy.

It seems to me, however, that the meaning of *ubuntu* is best captured in the isiXhosa expression *Umntu ngumntu ngabanye abantu*. Literally translated, this means, "A person is a person through being witnessed by, and engaging in reciprocal witnessing of other persons," or "A person becomes a human being through the multiplicity of relationships with others." The meaning conveyed by the expression is twofold. First, subjectivity depends on being witnessed; the richness of subjectivity flows from interconnectedness with the wider community, and from the reciprocal caring and complementarity of human relationships. Second, the phrase conveys the kind of reciprocity that calls on people to be ethical subjects. Mutual recognition is fundamental to being a fellow human being, a relational subject in the context of community. A person with *ubuntu* "is open and available to others, is affirming to others. . . . My humanity caught up, is inextricably bound up, in yours".[40]

---

40   Tutu, Desmond. 1999. No Future Without Forgiveness. New York: Doubleday.

Restoring Humanity after Historical Trauma: A Levinasian Vision

The examples presented in this essay from the traumatic apartheid past in South Africa, and from the Holocaust are illustrative of Emmanuel Levinas's philosophy of "ethical responsibility to the Other".[41] Levinas's ethics maintain that empathy is at the core of human subjectivity. Human subjectivity is realised by the encounter with the Other, and the face-to-face encounter is an ethical relation in which the subject "comprehends the Other through a discourse of 'response or responsibility.'"[42] When approached by the Other, one is confronted with the absolute otherness and precariousness of another, an otherness that escapes all comprehension. This precariousness and otherness is expressed in the face of the Other. It is not simply the face, but rather exposure, expression and the response elicited that matter. Adriaan Peperzak explains:

> When Levinas meditates on the significance of the face, he does not describe the complex figure that could be portrayed by a picture or painting; rather, he tries to make us 'experience' or 'realize' what we see, feel, 'know' when another, by looking at me, 'touches' me.[43]

Not only does Levinas's ethics maintain that subjectivity is realised by the encounter with the Other, but it also holds that the face-to-face encounter is an ethical relation in which the subject "comprehends the Other through a discourse of 'response or responsibility,' and understands the 'face' of the Other as an imperative 'demand.'"[44] Libin conceives of "response, responsiveness, responsibility" as the main condition on which the TRC's public hearings were predicated.[45] A failure to respond to the open hands extended by victims is a failure to recognise the call to responsibility issued by the face of the other; it is "to declare oneself unwilling to redress the wounds of the victims."[46] The TRC hearings constituted a platform on which the Other declared his or her presence while the act of testifying often involved "a literal staging of a performative 'face-to-face' encounter".[47] Libin argues further that the source of a victim's unspeakable trauma is located in the face of the Other. Consequently, in the face-to-face encoun-

---

41 Levinas, Emmanuel. 1969. Totality and Infinity: An Essay on Exteriority. Pittsburg: Duquesne University Press.

42 Levinas, Emmanuel. 1996. "Peace and Proximity." In Emmanuel Levinas: Basic Philosophical Writings, edited by Adriaan Peperzak, Simon Critchley and Robert Bernasconi, 162-167. Bloomington: Indiana University Press.

43 Peperzak, Adriaan T. 1993. To the Other: An Introduction to the Philosophy of Emmanuel Levinas. West Lafayette, IN: Purdue University Press.

44 Libin, Mark. 2007. "Can the subaltern be heard? Response and responsibility in South Africa's human spirit." Textual Practice 17: 119-127.

45 Ibid., 124.

46 Ibid., 127.

47 Ibid., 128.

ter, the victim "scrutinizes the face of the perpetrators in a search for significance, a desire to establish a relationship that will free [him/her] from trauma."[48]

The TRC was essentially a political project, the creation of a political compromise that played out in the public domain. Some may ask, is Levinas's ethics compatible with the political realm? Simon Critchley's introduction to Levina's essay, "Peace and Proximity" in an anthology of Levinas's work may be read as an answer to this question. Critchley notes that questions raised in response to Levinas's notion of ethics are often concerned with the relation between his ethics and "the spheres of reason, law, justice, and universality," i.e. politics.[49] However:

Photo: Bracha L Ettinger, CC BY-SA 2.5

Emmanuel Levinas (1906-1995)

> Levinas does not want to reject the order of political rationality and its consequent claims to universality and justice; rather, he wants to criticize the belief that only political rationality can answer political problems and to show how the order of the state rests upon the irreducible ethical responsibility of the face-to-face relation … [E]thics leads back to politics, to the demand of a just polity. Indeed, one might go further and claim that the ethical is ethical for the sake of politics, that is, for the sake of a transformed conception of politics and society.[50]

Indeed, in the discussion following his lecture "Transcendence and Height," Levinas posits that "both the hierarchy taught by Athens and the abstract and slightly anarchical ethical individualism taught by Jerusalem are simultaneously necessary in order to suppress violence. Each of these principles, left to itself, only furthers the contrary of what it wants to secure."[51]

These are precisely the ideas that were embodied in the TRC, which was nothing less than an effort to imbue the realms of law, justice and politics with a relational ethics that recognised the humanity of victims and perpetrators alike, "for the sake of a transformed conception of politics and society."[52]

---

48 Ibid, 128.
49 Critchley, Simon. "Introduction to 'Peace and Proximity.'" In Levinas: Basic Philosophical Writings, edited by Peperzak et al., 161.
50 Critchley, "Introduction," 161.
51 Peperzak, Adriaan T., Critchley, Simon and Bernasconi, Robert. 2008. Emmanuel Levinas: Basic Philosophical Writings. Bloomington: Indiana University Press.
52 Critchley, "Introduction", 161.

Conclusion

While the precept that one should respect and care for human beings as human beings is true, it has had little sway in curtailing atrocities or waves of vengeance following atrocities. It is as though "human being" – the face of the other – is too much of an abstraction (and, as the 20th century has shown, too pliable a notion). What is called for, it seems, is a movement from the abstract and the generalizable toward the particular and tangible; despite the fact that recognition of the particular does not necessarily guarantee compassion and empathy. The particular, especially when it is experienced as too particular, can just as easily result in contempt for the particular. Still, a thought or action that conveys a degree of particularity, which "rescues" the individual from and being completely obliterated by categories – especially those categories that lead to a negation of the other "as other," otherness "as unmitigated evil" which, Schrag and Paradiso-Michau explain, "reaches its most intense expression in ... genocide" – seems necessary for compassion and empathy to emerge.[53]

The work of psychoanalysts writing on the destructive effects of trauma on the development of victims' capacity for empathy[54] provides poignant support for the suggestion that victims may become so dehumanised that they lose the capacity for empathy. Yet, it also helps us to see that such a loss need not be permanent. Processes such as the TRC create the ethical space for empathic sensibilities damaged by violence both between individuals and within communities to be reanimated, making empathic human connection with former enemies possible.

My sense of how Levinas's ethics might be applied to an understanding of processes that lead to the emergence of empathy in encounters between victims and perpetrators, is that it is at the transcendence of vengefulness, where empathy, remorse and forgiveness are rendered possible albeit not inevitable. It is thus possible to conceive of an "in-between place" – a place between vengeance and forgiveness, to paraphrase Martha Minow.[55] It is almost as though the gazing upon the face of the other constitutes a moment of pause. As Levinas writes:

> The Other, whose exceptional presence is inscribed in the ethical impossibility of killing him in which I stand, marks the end of [my] powers .... Morality begins when freedom, instead of being justified by itself, feels itself to be arbitrary and violent.[56]

53 Schrag, Calvin O., and Michael Paradiso-Michau. 2012. Reflections in the Religious, the Ethical, and the Political. New York: Lexington Books.

54 Laub, Dori and Nanette C. Auerhuhn. 1989. "Failed empathy: A central theme in the survivor's Holocaust experience." Psychoanalytic Psychology 6: 377-400.

55 Minow, Martha. 1999. Between vengeance and forgiveness: Facing history after genocide and mass violence. Boston: Beacon Press.

56 Levinas, Totality and Infinity, 87.

Morality begins when freedom – including the freedom to avenge a wrong committed against one – is questioned. This goal can be attained through the face-to-face encounter between former enemies, and through dialogue. Managed carefully, this kind of dialogue can help victims, perpetrators and the descendants of these groups to take first steps into the light of hopefulness – hope, not as an abstract concept, but as a moment imbued with the real possibility of deepening a sense of acknowledgement, understanding and respect for the Other's pain and suffering in the pasts, and together participate in living reconciliation.

Pumla Gobodo-Madikizela

The Claude Ake Visiting Chair and Memorial Paper

The Claude Ake Visiting Chair was set up in 2003 at the Department of Peace and Conflict Research, Uppsala University (DPCR), in collaboration with the Nordic Africa Institute (NAI) and with funding from the Swedish Government and Uppsala University. The Chair honours the memory of Professor Claude Ake, a distinguished scholar, philosopher, teacher and humanist, who died tragically in 1996. The Chair is intended for scholars who, like Claude Ake, combine a profound commitment to scholarship with a strong advocacy for social justice.

The Chair is open to social scientists working at African universities with problems related to war, peace, conflict resolution, human rights, democracy and development on the African continent. The visiting chair holder is offered a conducive environment to pursue his or her own research, while there is also opportunity for lecturing, holding seminars and contributing to ongoing research activities at the Department of Peace and Conflict Research and the Nordic Africa Institute.

The holders of the Claude Ake Visiting Chair give, at the end of their stay in Uppsala, a public 'Claude Ake Memorial Lecture.' The title, theme and content of the lecture should be based on the research project being pursued by the chair holder while in Uppsala. The topic of the lecture shall, in a general sense, relate to the work of Claude Ake, for example in terms of themes or issues covered, or in the theoretical or normative points of departure. The lecture is based on a paper prepared and made available to seminar participants and lecture audience in advance of the lecture. The paper is subsequently published jointly by DPCR and NAI.

CLAUDE AKE MEMORIAL PAPERS

1. JINADU, L. Adele; Explaining and Managing Ethnic Conflict in Africa: Towards a Cultural Theory of Democracy (2007)

2. OBI, Cyril I.; No Choice, But Democracy: Prising the People out of Politics in Africa? (2008)

3. SESAY, Amadu; The African Union: Forward March or About Face-Turn? (2008)

4. BOAFO-ARTHUR, Kwame; Democracy and Stability in West Africa: The Ghanaian Experience (2008)

5. VILLA-VICENCIO, Charles; Where the Old Meets the New: Transitional Justice, Peacebuilding and Traditional Reconciliation Practices in Africa (2009)

6. MOHAMED, Adam Azzain; Evaluating the Darfur Peace Agreement: A Call for an Alternative Approach to Crisis Management

7. MBABAZI, Pamela K; The Oil Industry in Uganda: A Blessing in Disguise or an all Too Familiar Curse? (2013)

8. ADETULA, Victor A.O.; African Conflicts, Development and Regional Organisations in the Post-Cold War International System (2015)

9. GOBODO-MADIKIZELA, Pumla; What Does It Mean to be Human in the Aftermath of Historical Trauma? Re-envisioning The Sunflower and Why Hannah Arendt was Wrong (2016)

All of these titles can be found in full text for open access at the online research publication database DiVA at www.diva-portal.org

www.ingramcontent.com/pod-product-compliance
Lightning Source LLC
Chambersburg PA
CBHW041429270326
41933CB00024B/3493